D0230016

60000382964

infographic
HOW IT WORKS

TODAY'S TECHNOLOGY

WAYLAND

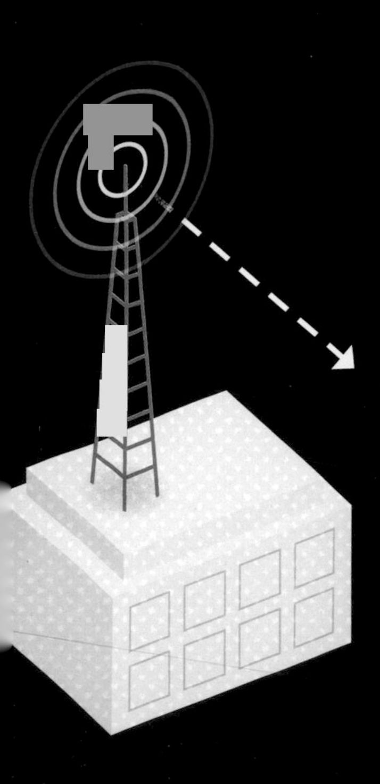

First published in Great Britain
in 2016 by Wayland

Editor: Liza Miller
Produced by Tall Tree Ltd
Editor: Jon Richards
Designer: Ed Simkins

ISBN: 978 0 7502 9932 9
10 9 8 7 6 5 4 3 2 1

Wayland
An imprint of Hachette
Children's Group
Part of Hodder and Stoughton
Carmelite House
50 Victoria Embankment
London EC4Y 0DZ

An Hachette UK Company
www.hachette.co.uk
www.hachettechildrens.co.uk

Printed and bound in China

CONTENTS

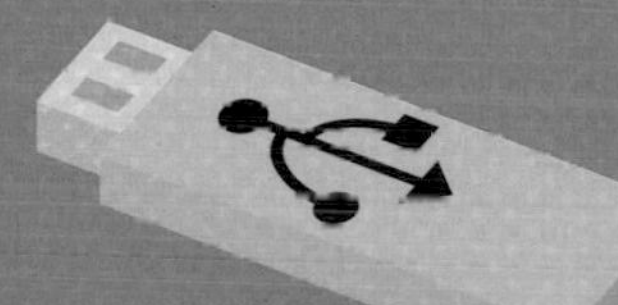

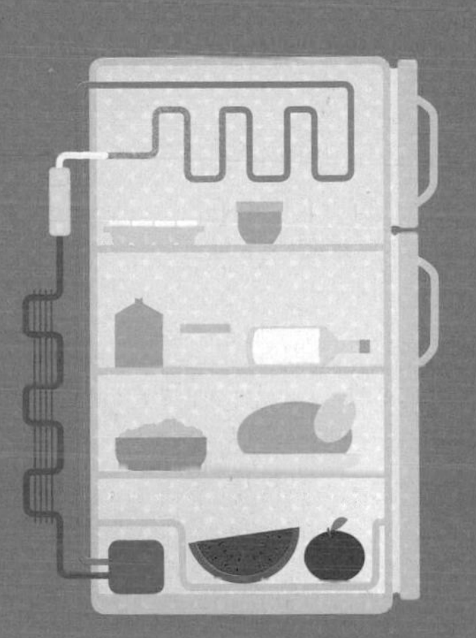

TECHNO WONDERS

Humans have always developed ideas to make our lives easier and more comfortable, whether using fire to cook food, creating wheels to move loads or high-tech ways of sending data to the other side of the globe. This book will look at some of the technological wonders of the modern world, showing how they work and how they make our lives better.

INFO TECH

The internet allows us to send and receive information in a wide range of formats and over huge distances. Since 2000, the number of people around the world who have access to the internet has grown from about 394 million to over 3 billion today. How we interact with the Web has changed dramatically in recent years, with more and more people using mobile internet connections on phones and tablets, instead of desktop computers.

394 MILLION

2000

TODAY

3 BILLION

2011

TODAY

Globally, there are nearly 2.5 billion mobile broadband subscriptions. That's double the number it was in 2011.

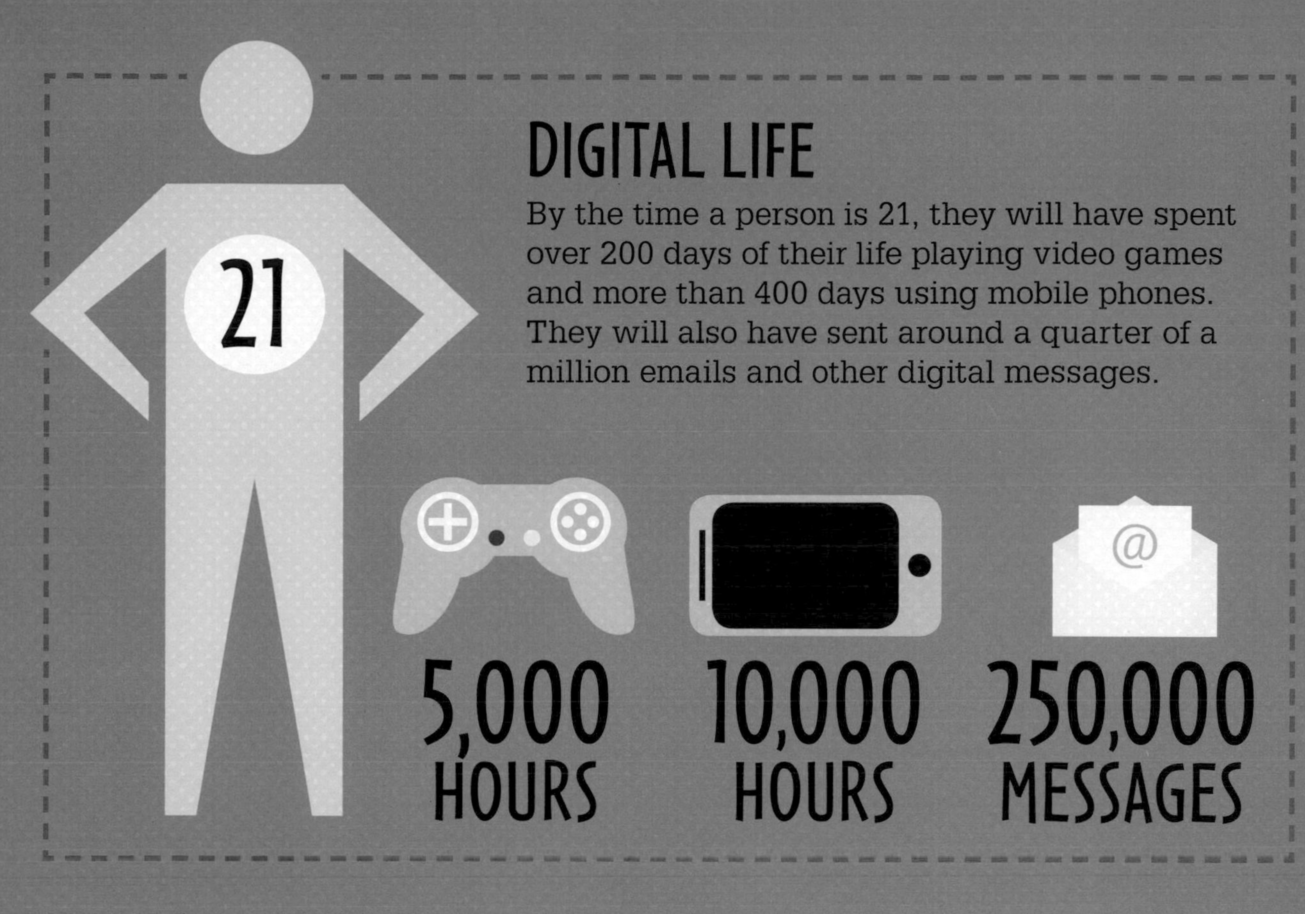

DIGITAL LIFE

By the time a person is 21, they will have spent over 200 days of their life playing video games and more than 400 days using mobile phones. They will also have sent around a quarter of a million emails and other digital messages.

TECH WASTE

As technology improves and devices get better, people tend to dispose of older, unwanted gadgets. For example, every year, people around the world get rid of 50 million tonnes of computers and digital devices – that's more than eight times the weight of the Great Pyramid of Giza!

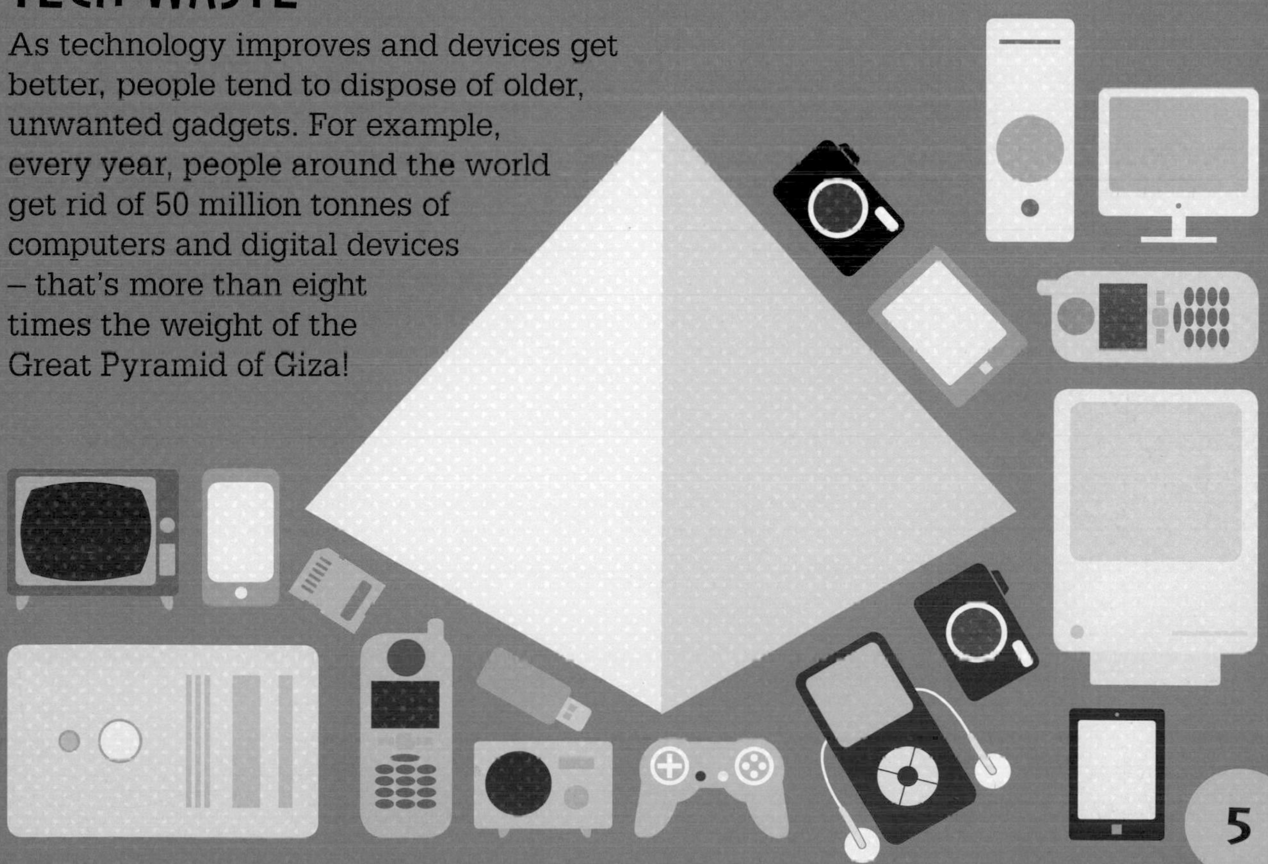

HOW A HOUSE CAN MAKE ITS OWN POWER

Many homes today get their power from the mains gas and electricity supplies. However, producing this power creates pollution. Today, it is possible to build or convert a house so that it can provide for all of its own power needs using non-polluting methods.

1 ON THE ROOF

Solar panels on the roof use energy from the sun in one of two ways. Photovoltaic cells convert sunlight into electricity, while another type uses the sun's heat to warm water flowing through pipes inside them.

sun

solar panels

Triple-glazed windows help keep the heat in.

2 UNDERGROUND

Just below the surface, the ground stays at a constant temperature all-year round. Ground source heat pumps push water through pipes buried in the ground to collect this heat, which can be used to warm the house or heat up water.

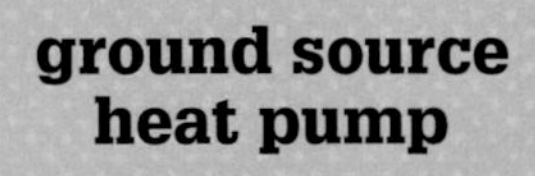

TRY THIS ...

Design an electricity generating system for your school. Think about which method or methods would work best and where they could be located to produce the most energy. Does your school have a windy spot for a wind turbine, or a large sunny area for solar cells?

wind turbine

Another method of energy generation is to burn the bio-gas produced by rotting food and manure.

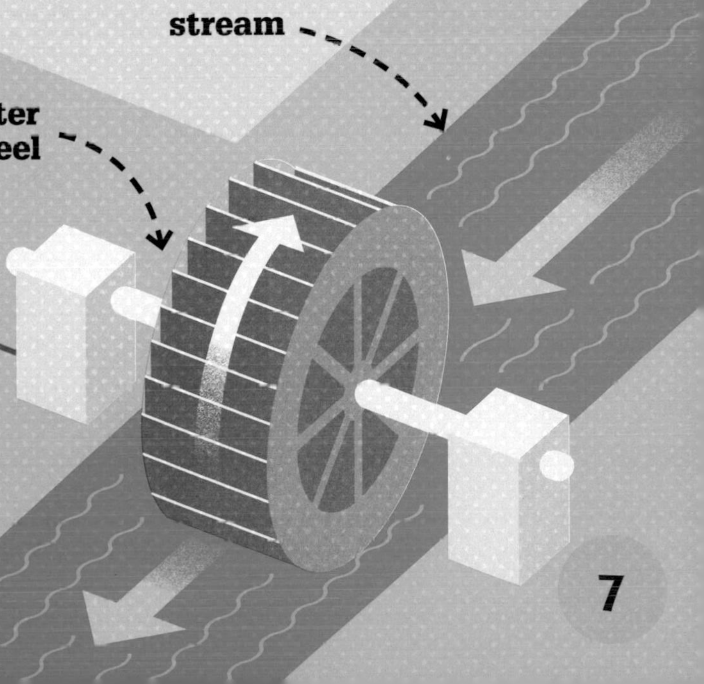

3 WIND POWER

A turbine spins when the wind blows to turn a generator and produce electricity. The turbine can stand on its own mast or it can be attached to the roof.

stream

water wheel

4 WATER

Houses that stand near a stream or river can use the flowing water to spin a turbine attached to a generator to produce electricity.

HOW A LIGHT BULB GLOWS

Before the invention of the light bulb, people had to burn candles or light gas lamps to see in the dark. Today, we can flick a switch and turn on a bright, low-energy LED (light-emitting diode) that produces an energy-efficient light.

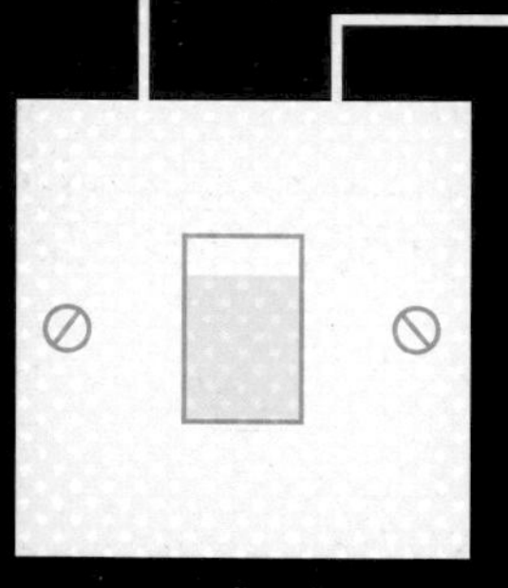

1 SWITCH

When you flick a light switch, electricity passes along wires and into the LED bulb.

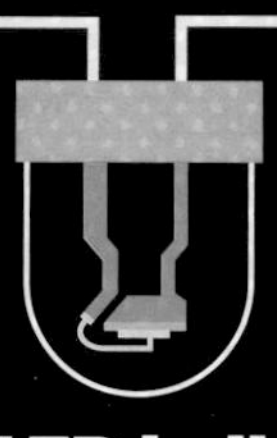

2 DIODES

Inside the LED is a diode. This contains two parts. One part, called the p-type, has few electrons but lots of 'electron holes', while the other part, called the n-type, has extra electrons.

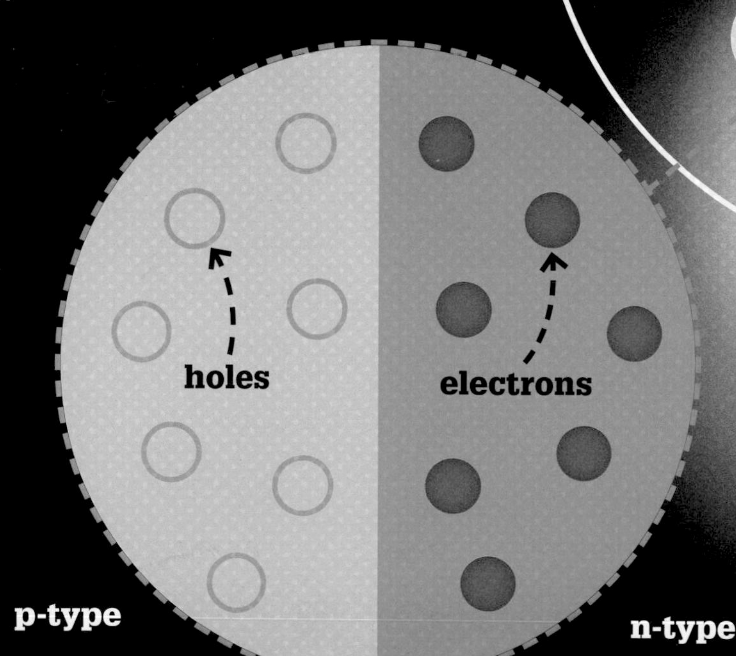

LED lights last up to 50 times longer than traditional light bulbs.

TRY THIS ...

If a traditional light bulb could last for 1,200 hours, how long will a modern LED bulb last for?

A traditional light bulb features a small, tightly wound coil inside the glass bulb. The coil glows as electricity moves through it. However, this type of light bulb is very inefficient, as a lot of the energy it produces (up to 90 per cent) is released as heat instead of light.

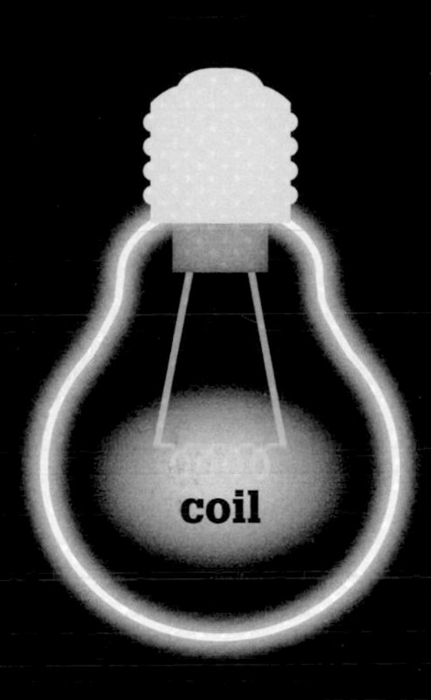

case

diode

3 FLOW

When electricity flows through these two parts, it pushes electrons into the p-type part and electron holes into the n-type part.

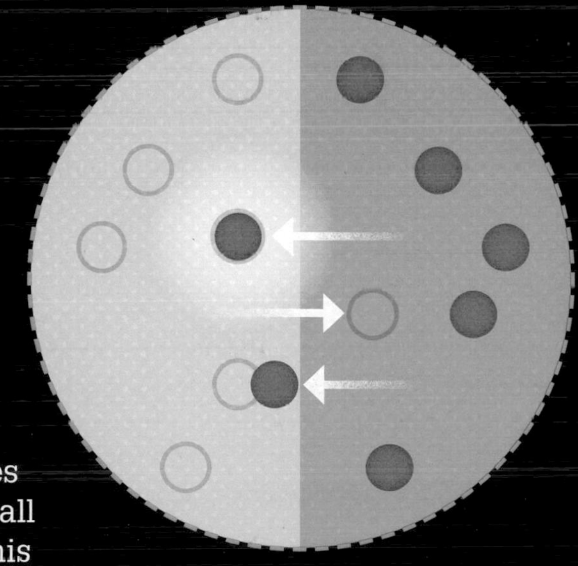

4 MAKING LIGHT

The electrons combine with the electron holes to make complete atoms. This produces a small amount of energy that is released as light. This type of reaction is called electroluminescence.

HOW A MICROWAVE COOKS FOOD

Normal ovens cook food by heating air using a gas-fuelled flame or an element that glows red-hot when electricity passes through it. However, a microwave oven uses radiation to heat food from the inside out.

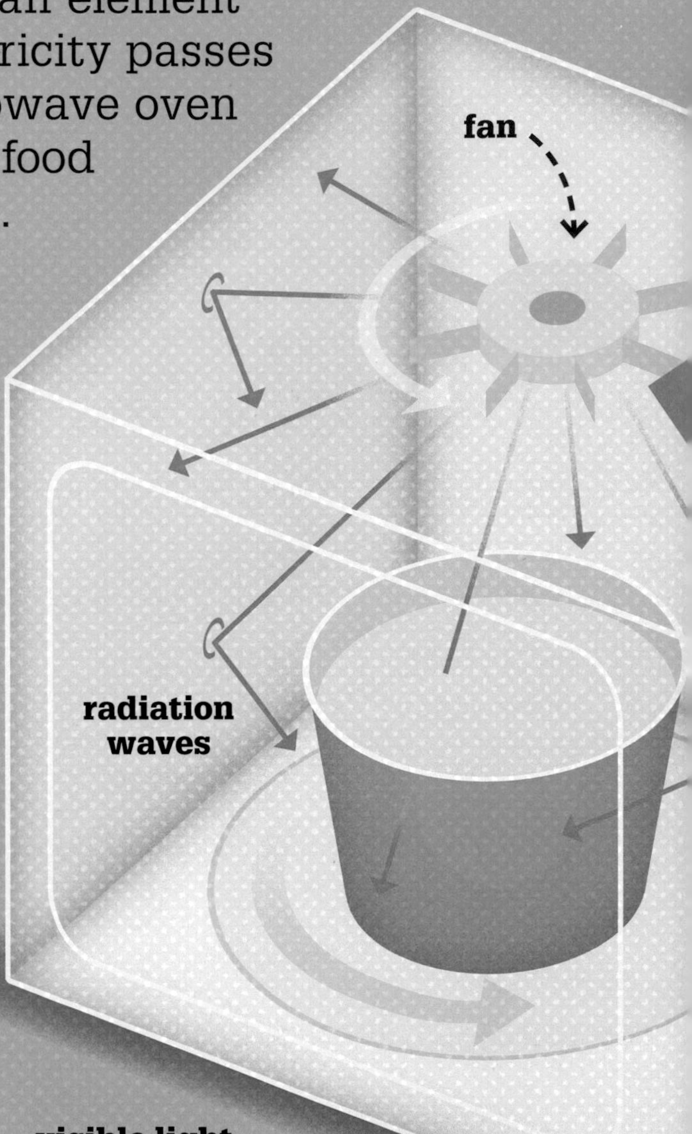

1 MAKING WAVES

Inside a microwave oven is a device which produces microwave radiation. This device is called a magnetron.

2 SCATTERING

After the waves of radiation leave the magnetron, they are scattered about the inside of the microwave by the shiny blades of a spinning fan.

Microwaves form part of the electromagnetic spectrum, which also includes visible light, radio waves and X-rays.

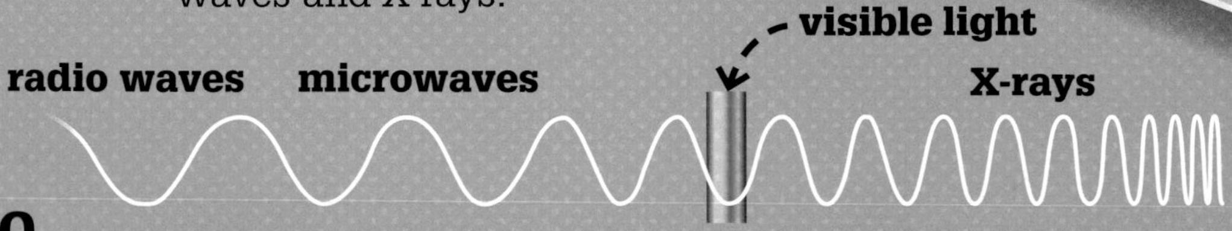

TRY THIS ...

A frozen meal takes 5 minutes to defrost in a microwave, 6.5 minutes to cook properly and another minute to stand. Work out the total amount of time in seconds it takes to prepare the meal.

3 BOUNCING WAVES

The radiation also bounces off the inside walls of the oven, so that all parts of the food receive a similar dose of radiation.

4 VIBRATING

As the waves of radiation pass through the food, they cause water particles in it to vibrate.

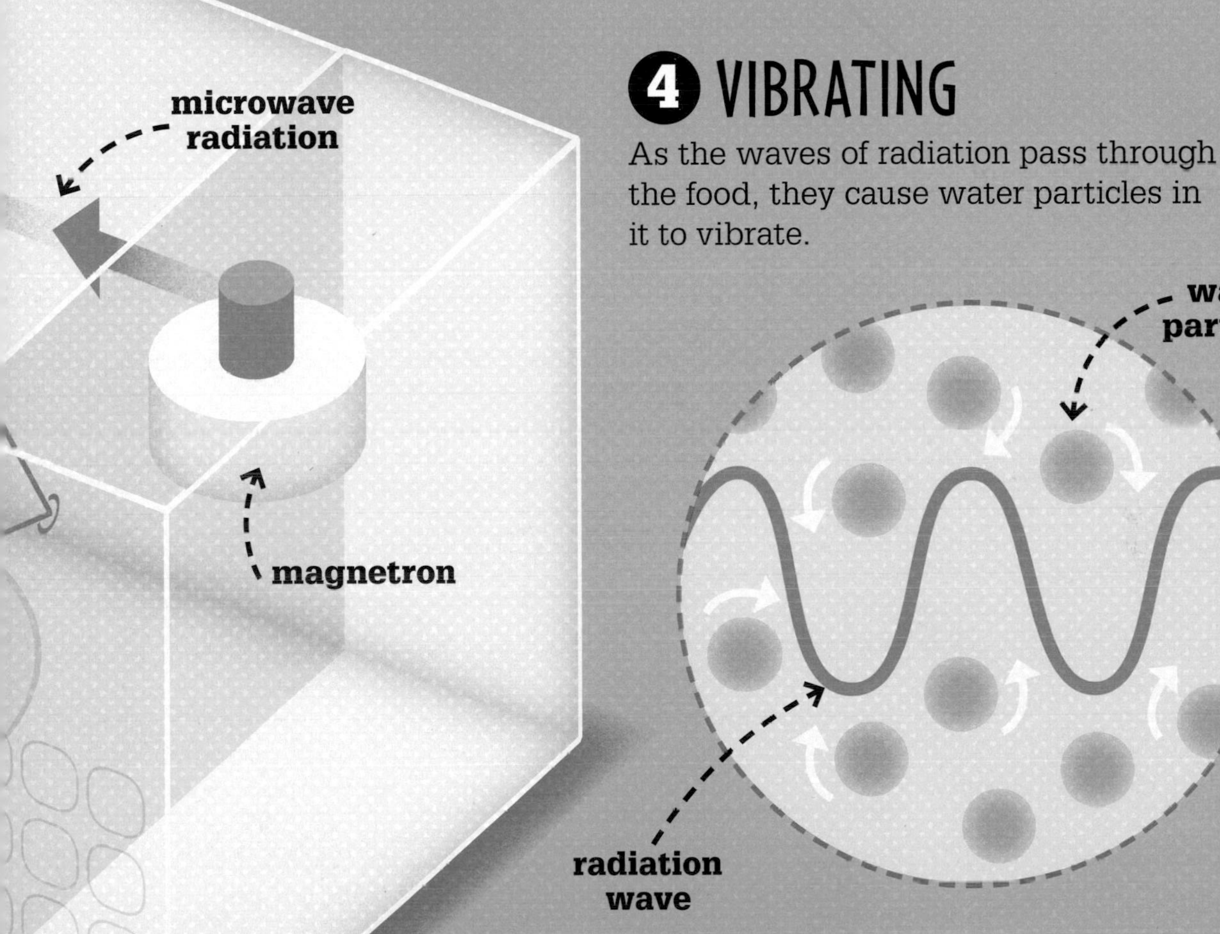

5 COOKING

As the particles vibrate, they produce heat inside the food, cooking it from within.

HOW A REFRIGERATOR KEEPS FOOD FRESH

Keeping food cool slows down the activity of any bacteria that may attack it and cause it to go bad. We keep food in a fridge so it stays fresher for longer than it would do if it were left at room temperature.

1 PIPE NETWORK

A pipe runs through the inside and outside of the fridge. Inside this pipe is a special chemical called a refrigerant.

2 EXPANDING

As the pipe enters the fridge, it passes through a valve that expands the refrigerant. Since expanding gases cool down, the refrigerant entering the fridge is cold.

3 CHILLING

The cold refrigerant absorbs heat from inside the fridge, making the inside of the fridge cooler.

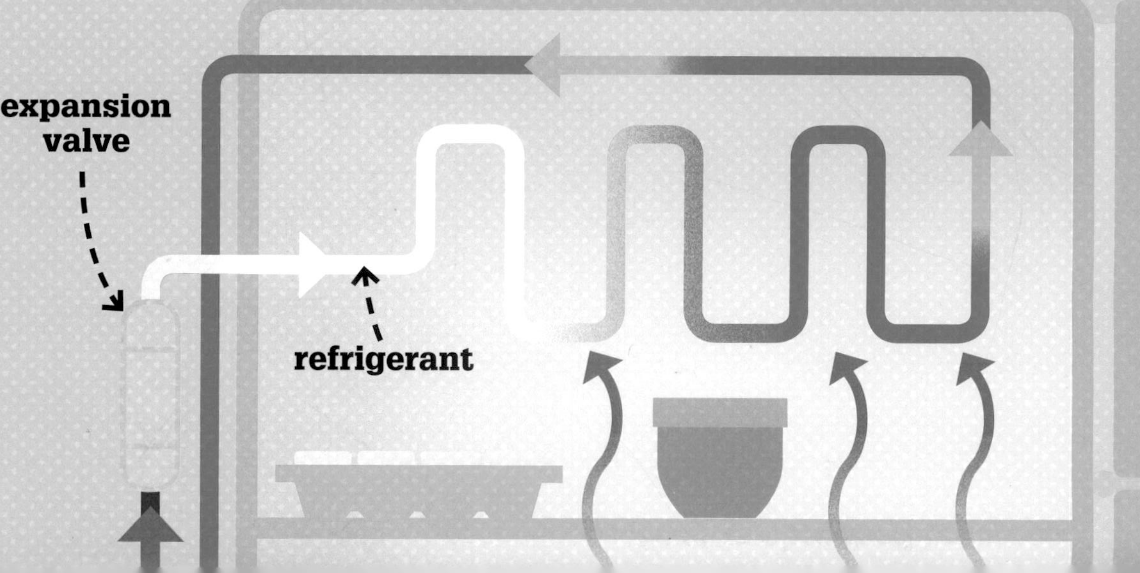

4 SQUEEZING

As the refrigerant flows out of the fridge, it passes through an electric pump called a compressor, which squeezes the refrigerant and causes it to heat up.

5 COOLING

The compressed refrigerant then passes through a network of thin pipes called a condenser, where heat from the refrigerant is released into the outside air.

6 BACK AGAIN

The refrigerant passes back into the fridge and the cycle continues, taking more and more heat out of the fridge, until it reaches the temperature set by the fridge's thermostat.

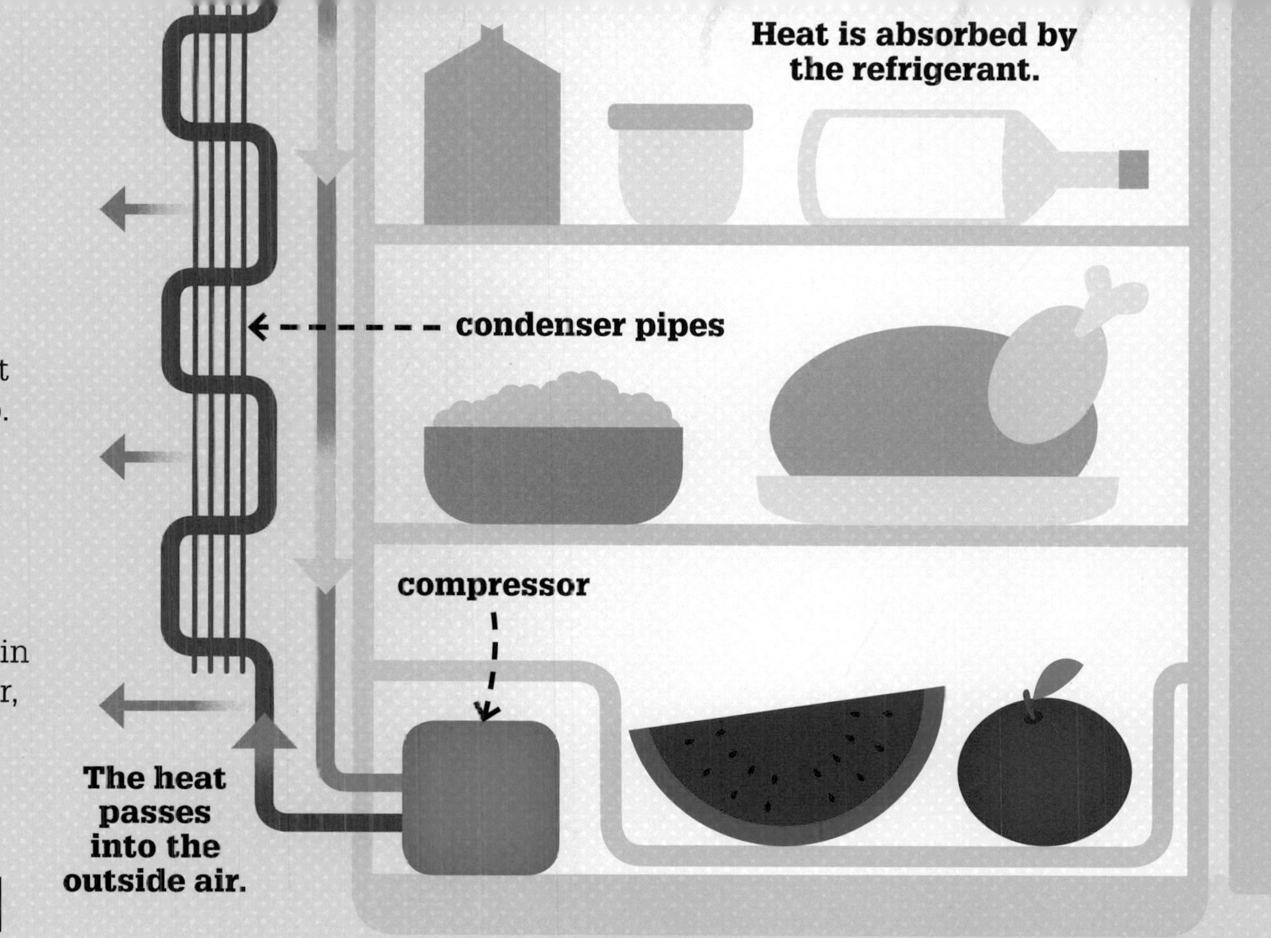

TRY THIS ...

Pump up a tyre on a bicycle. The pumping action squeezes the air, which should make it heat up. Feel the nozzle of the pump. Does it feel warm or cold?

HOW A ROBOT CLEANS A ROOM

Robot vacuum cleaners use rotating brushes and suction to remove dirt, just like a normal vacuum cleaner. However, they can go about their work without human direction, avoiding obstacles and guiding themselves around objects.

1 ROBOT SENSORS

A robot vacuum cleaner has a variety of sensors around its body, including infrared sensors. These send out beams of invisible light that detect any reflections which bounce off walls and other obstacles, so the robot knows that it is approaching something.

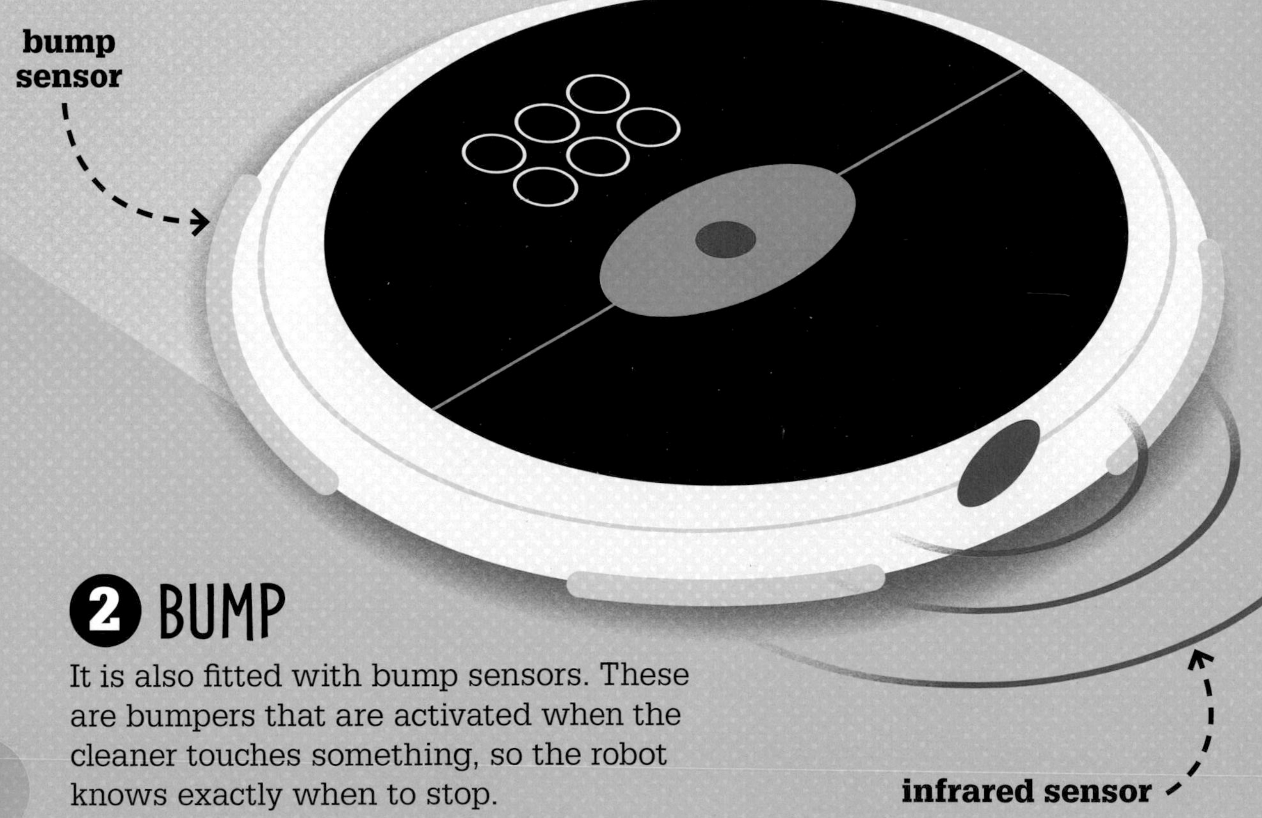

2 BUMP

It is also fitted with bump sensors. These are bumpers that are activated when the cleaner touches something, so the robot knows exactly when to stop.

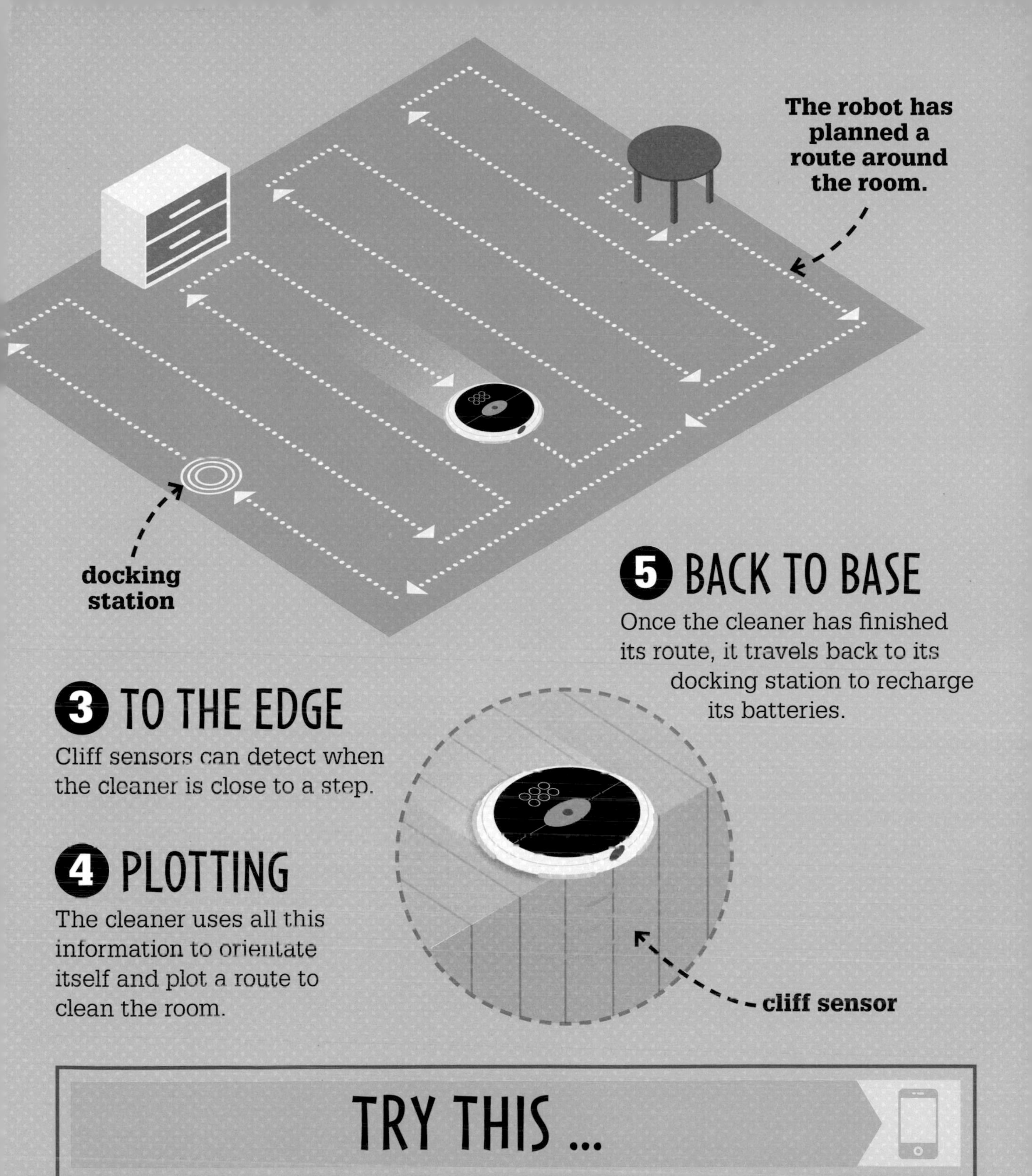

5 BACK TO BASE

Once the cleaner has finished its route, it travels back to its docking station to recharge its batteries.

3 TO THE EDGE

Cliff sensors can detect when the cleaner is close to a step.

4 PLOTTING

The cleaner uses all this information to orientate itself and plot a route to clean the room.

TRY THIS ...

Using graph paper, make a scale drawing of a room in your home and plan a route that a robot vacuum cleaner could take. Can you plot the shortest route to clean all of the floor?

HOW TV IS BROADCAST

Millions of us around the world spend hours every week watching television shows that are sent directly to TV sets in our homes. But how do these shows travel the many kilometres to reach where you live?

1 RECORDING

TV cameras record an image of what's in front of them. They record images 24 times or more per second – so fast that the human eye interprets them as moving pictures.

2 PICTURE LINES

Light detectors inside the camera record each image as a series of hundreds of lines.

Images are recorded by camera.

3 SOUND

At the same time, microphones record any sounds that go with the picture.

4 TRANSMITTING

The pictures and sounds are converted into radio signals and passed on to a transmitter.

TRY THIS ...

A high-speed TV camera will record 250 frames a second. How many more frames will it record over 5 seconds compared to a normal camera that records 24 frames per second?

satellite

radio signal

A repeater tower passes on the signal.

5 SIGNALS

The transmitter sends out radio signals that are collected by aerials on your home. Alternatively, the signals may be sent to a satellite and beamed to a satellite dish on your home. The signals can also travel along a fibre-optic cable.

fibre-optic cable

aerial

satellite dish

6 AT HOME

Once the signals have reached your home, they are carried along cables to your TV set where you can see the pictures and hear the sounds.

HOW A COMPUTER WORKS

Computers and computer processors are found in many electrical devices we use every day, from smartphones and tablets to cars, fridges and even dishwashers. Despite this range of devices, all computers operate in the same way.

1 INPUT DEVICES

The flow of information to a computer starts with the input device. This can be a keyboard or mouse on a computer, a touchscreen on a tablet, or the buttons on the front of a washing machine.

2 PROCESSING

The information passes to the computer processor. This decides what the device should then do, based on the software that the device is running.

The term hardware refers to the parts of a computer, while the term software refers to the programs that a computer runs, telling it what to do.

TRY THIS ...

If a computer's hard drive has a capacity, or limit, of 528 gigabytes, how many movies can it store, if each movie is 4 gigabytes?

5 EXTERNAL

Some computers also have removable storage devices, such as flash memory cards. Files can be saved on to this without taking up space in the computer's storage.

hard drive

4 STORAGE

A computer will also have storage on its hard drive where you can keep your files, such as photos, movies or typed documents.

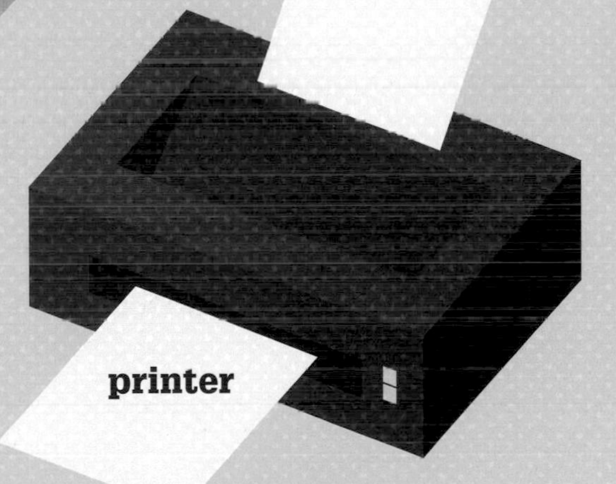

screen

speakers

3 OUTPUT DEVICES

An output device then displays what is happening. This could be the screen on your computer to show graphics, speakers to play sounds or a printer to produce a paper copy.

HOW MUSIC AND MOVIES ARE STREAMED

The internet allows us to view web pages and access information from anywhere on the planet. It also lets us stream content, so that we can listen to the latest music and watch films and TV programmes instantly.

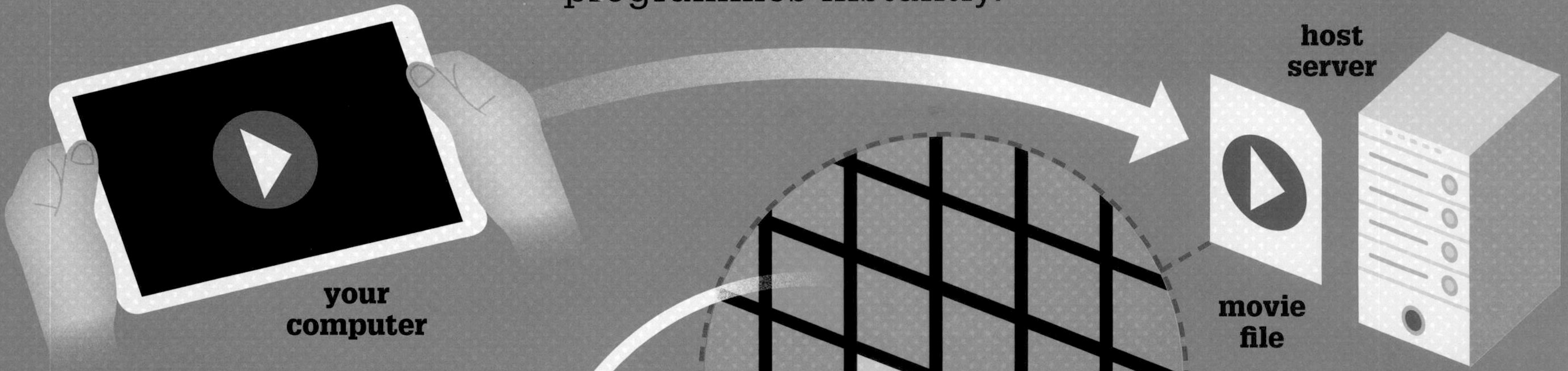

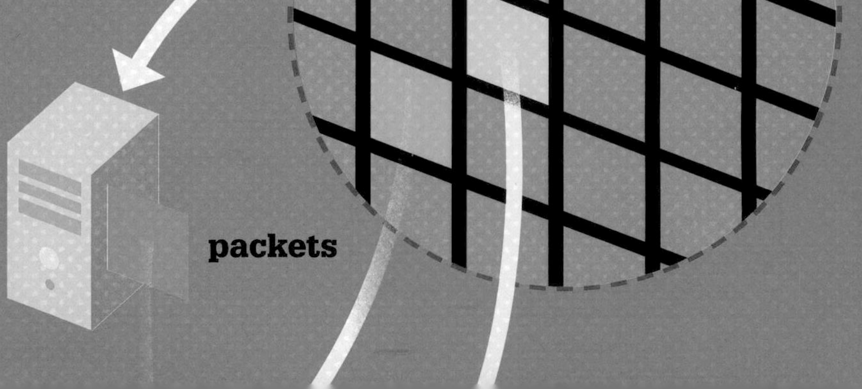

your computer

host server

movie file

packets

1 SERVER

To let you stream a movie, your computer or web browser accesses another computer hard drive, called a server, where a film is stored.

2 PACKETS

The server breaks up a movie file into smaller pieces, called packets.

3 DIFFERENT ROUTES

The server sends these packets over the internet to your computer. Because the internet is made up of billions of connections around the world, each packet can travel using a completely different route.

Your web browser has a temporary area of memory storage called a cache. The packets are stored in the cache as they arrive and are put together.

4 PUT IT BACK

As each packet arrives, your computer starts to put them back together in the order they indicate. The progress bar in your browser shows how much of a file you've viewed, and how much has been downloaded into its cache.

The computer puts the packets back together.

5 WATCHING

When enough of the file has arrived, the movie starts to play. Meanwhile, more packets arrive. As each one is viewed, it is deleted by your computer, leaving room for more in your browser's cache.

TRY THIS ...

Try streaming the same movie at your home and at school (always ask an adult's permission before you do this). Look at the progress bar and time how long the movie takes to download into the cache. Is it faster at school or at home?

HOW A MOBILE PHONE SENDS CALLS

Today, there are more mobile phones on the planet than people. These small devices allow us to make calls from almost anywhere, as long as we are near a cell phone mast that can send and receive signals to and from our phones.

1 CELLS

A geographical region is divided into hexagonal areas called cells, inside each of which is a phone mast.

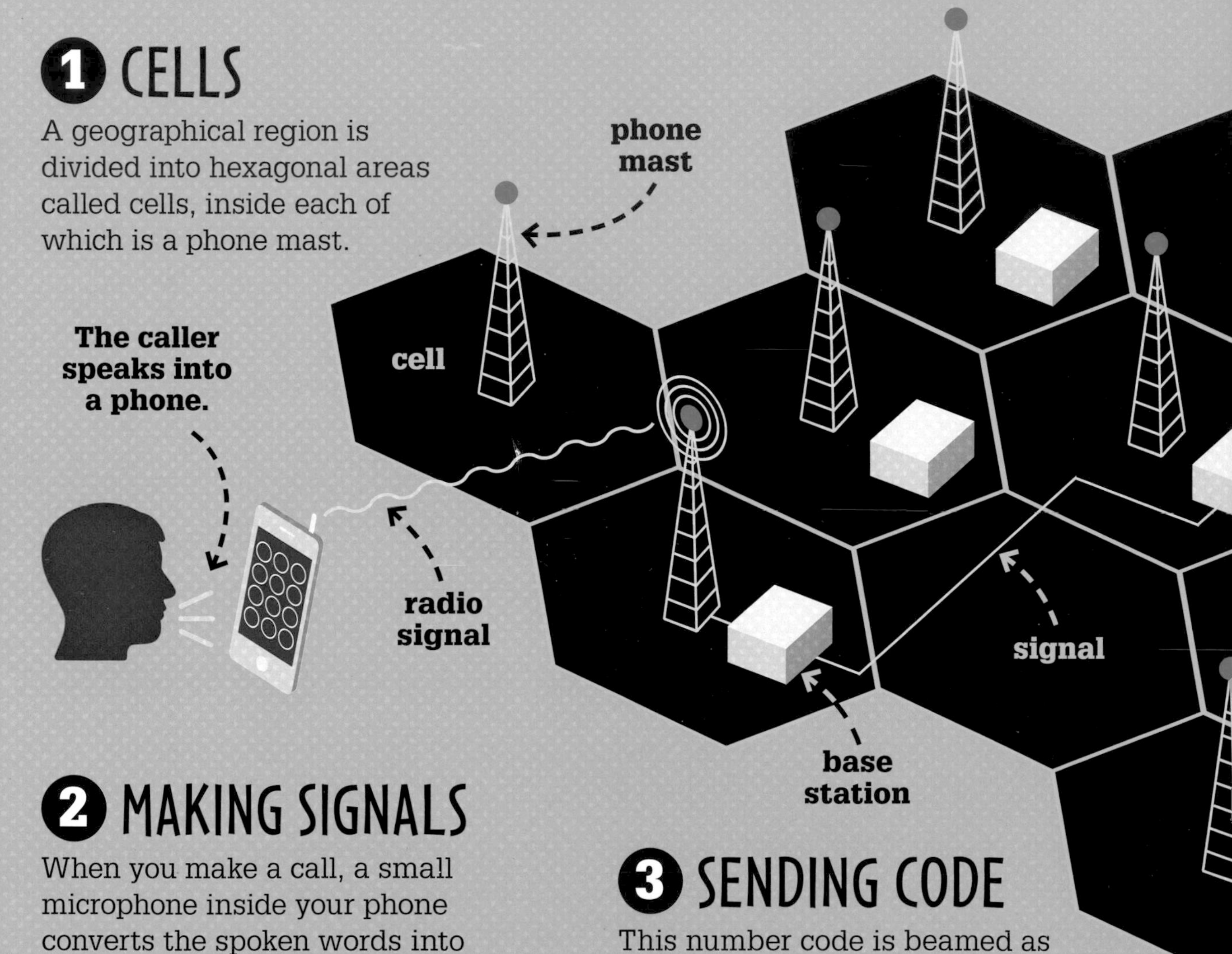

2 MAKING SIGNALS

When you make a call, a small microphone inside your phone converts the spoken words into an electrical signal. The phone converts this into a code of numbers.

3 SENDING CODE

This number code is beamed as a radio signal from an aerial or antenna in your phone.

TRY THIS ...

If the signal of a phone call travels at about 300,000 km/s, calculate how long it would take in seconds for an international phone message to travel between two callers who are 9,000 km apart.

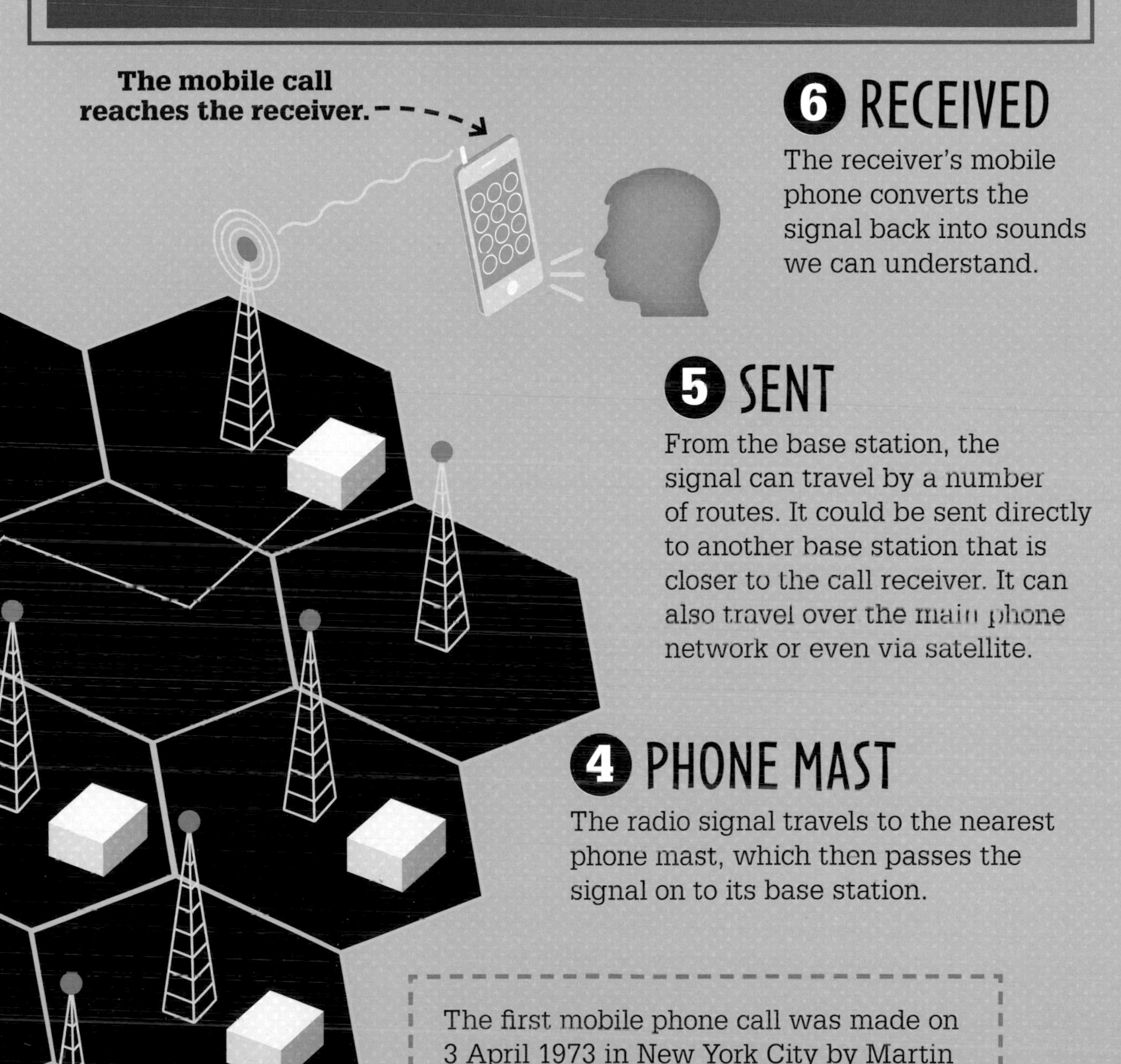

6 RECEIVED

The receiver's mobile phone converts the signal back into sounds we can understand.

5 SENT

From the base station, the signal can travel by a number of routes. It could be sent directly to another base station that is closer to the call receiver. It can also travel over the main phone network or even via satellite.

4 PHONE MAST

The radio signal travels to the nearest phone mast, which then passes the signal on to its base station.

The first mobile phone call was made on 3 April 1973 in New York City by Martin Cooper. The phone he used was the size of a brick and weighed about 1 kg!

HOW A TOUCHSCREEN WORKS

Touch-sensitive screens, or touchscreens, let us input information or interact with devices simply by touching a screen, rather than using a computer mouse. There are two main types of touchscreen and they are found on many devices, including smartphones.

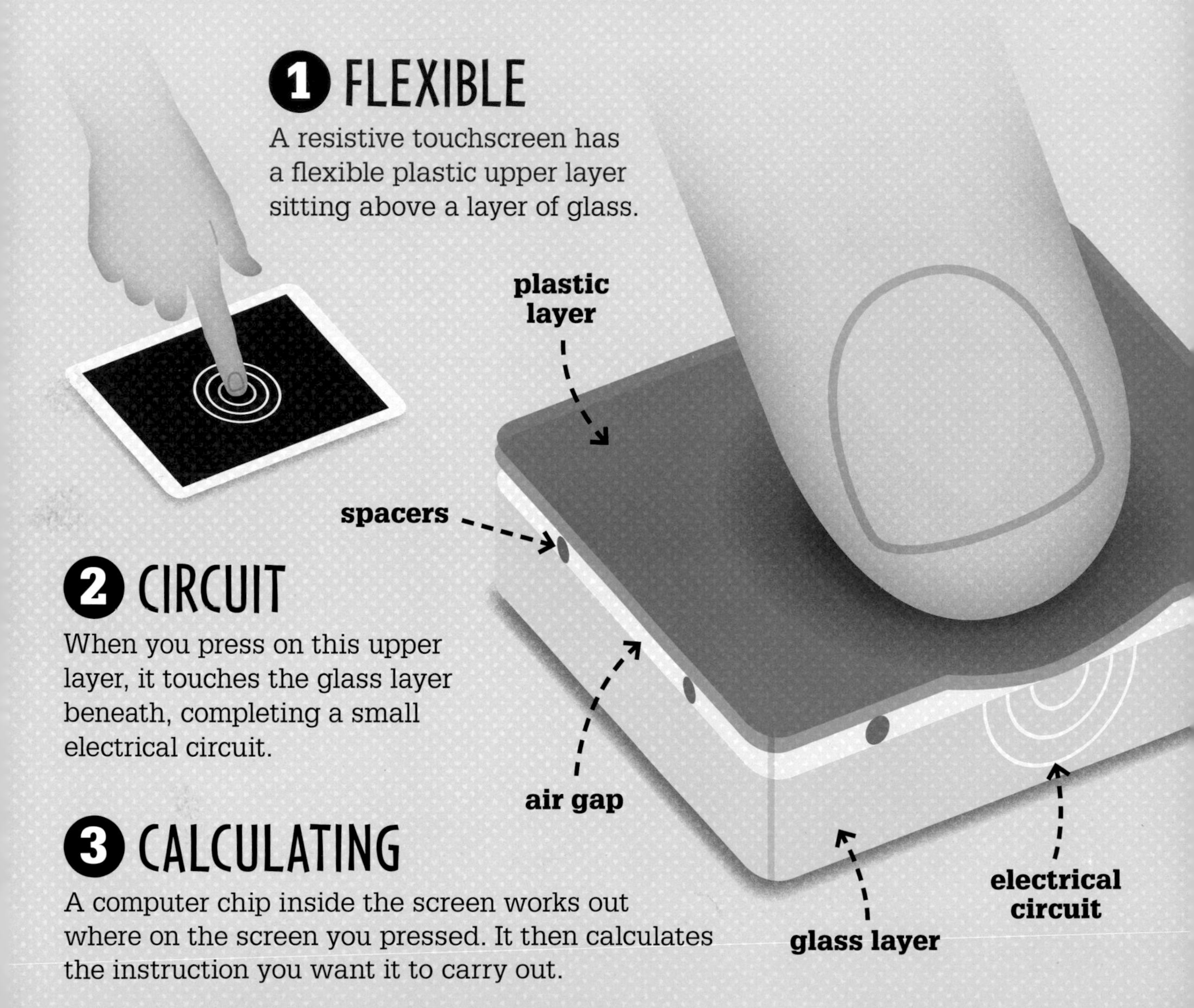

1 FLEXIBLE

A resistive touchscreen has a flexible plastic upper layer sitting above a layer of glass.

2 CIRCUIT

When you press on this upper layer, it touches the glass layer beneath, completing a small electrical circuit.

3 CALCULATING

A computer chip inside the screen works out where on the screen you pressed. It then calculates the instruction you want it to carry out.

Resistive touchscreens can only be touched in one place, whereas capacitive touchscreens can support multiple touches. Smartphones are fitted with capacitive screens.

1 ELECTRICAL FIELD

A capacitive touchscreen is made up of layers of glass that conduct electricity and create an electrical field.

2 CHANGING FIELD

When you touch the outer screen, you alter the electrical field depending on where your finger is.

3 WHAT TO DO

A computer chip detects where this happens on a screen and calculates which instructions you want it to carry out.

TRY THIS ...

Make a list of devices around your home, school and town that have touchscreens. Can you work out which of these devices use capacitive screens and which use resistive ones?

HOW GPS FINDS YOU

Orbiting Earth is a squadron of satellites that make up the Global Positioning System (GPS). These send out signals so that we can find out where we are. In the right conditions, it can do this job to within a few metres.

GPS satellites

coded signal

1 IN ORBIT

Wherever you are on Earth, there will usually be several satellites in space above your head. These satellites are continually sending signals to Earth.

2 CODED SIGNALS

The signals have a special code to identify each satellite and the precise time they left the satellite. Because they are radio signals, they travel at the speed of light.

There are 24 GPS satellites in orbit around Earth at an altitude of about 19,000 km.

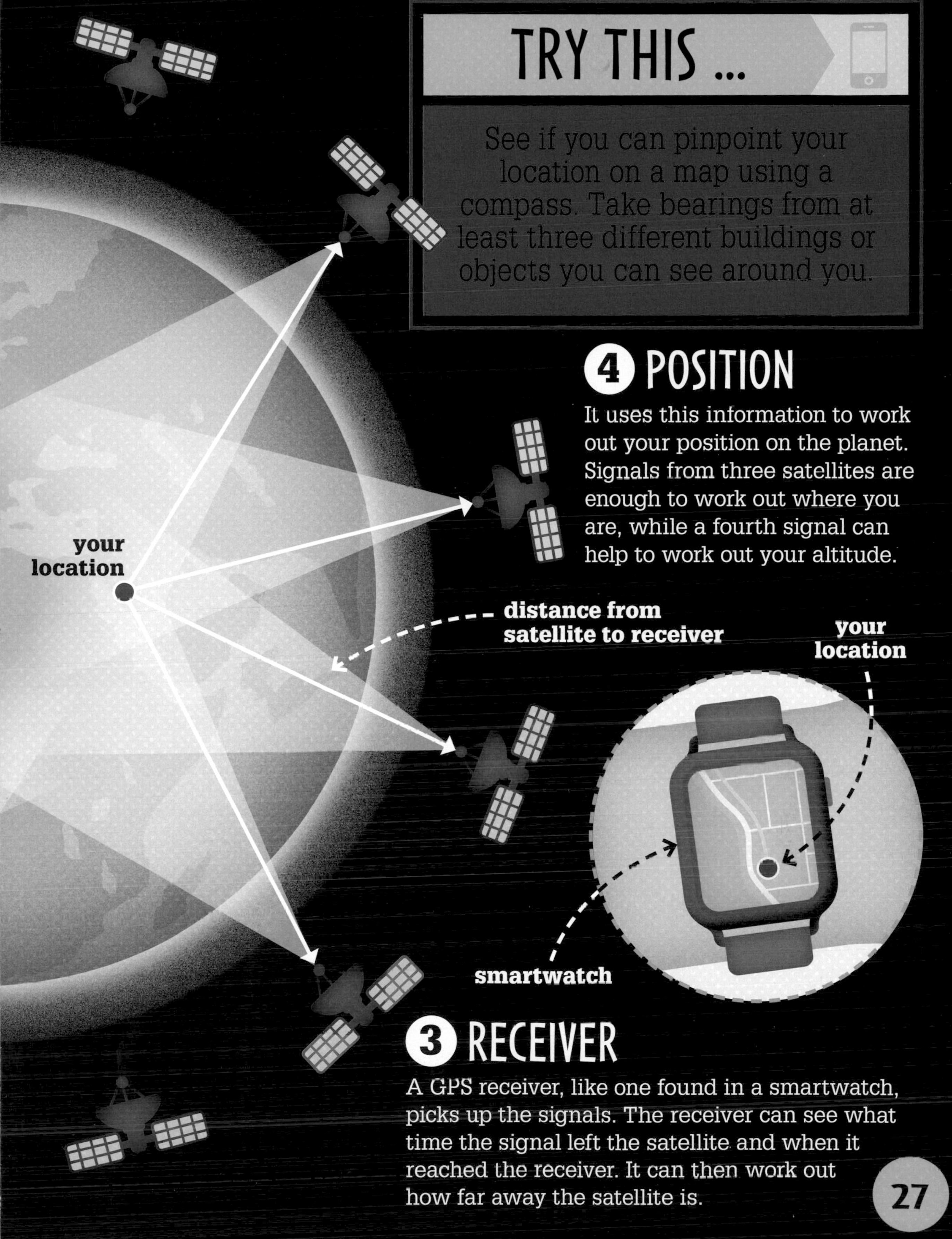

TRY THIS ...

See if you can pinpoint your location on a map using a compass. Take bearings from at least three different buildings or objects you can see around you.

4 POSITION

It uses this information to work out your position on the planet. Signals from three satellites are enough to work out where you are, while a fourth signal can help to work out your altitude.

3 RECEIVER

A GPS receiver, like one found in a smartwatch, picks up the signals. The receiver can see what time the signal left the satellite and when it reached the receiver. It can then work out how far away the satellite is.

HOW A 3-D PRINTER WORKS

Traditionally, if you wanted to make a model of something, you would carve it from a solid block of wood, plastic or metal. This would mean chipping away pieces to create the model you were after, leaving you with a lot of unwanted material. However, 3-D printers can create new objects without producing any waste.

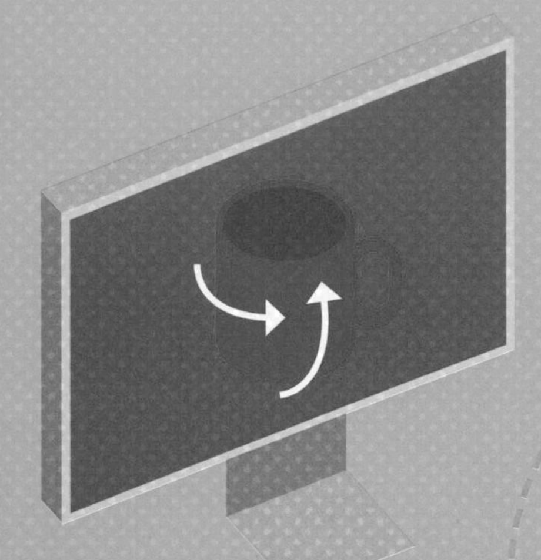

1 DIGITAL MODEL

A computer is used to create a digital model of the object you want to make.

Plastic is fed in through a tube.

2 SLICES

A program will then break the model up into horizontal slices.

3 PRINTING

Instructions for each slice are then sent to the printer, which starts the printing.

TRY THIS ...

Take an everyday object, such as a shoe or a ball. Can you draw some of the slices that would make up a 3-D model of that object?

4 FUSING

The printer builds each slice by feeding molten plastic or powder through its nozzle and fusing it together using glue or ultraviolet light.

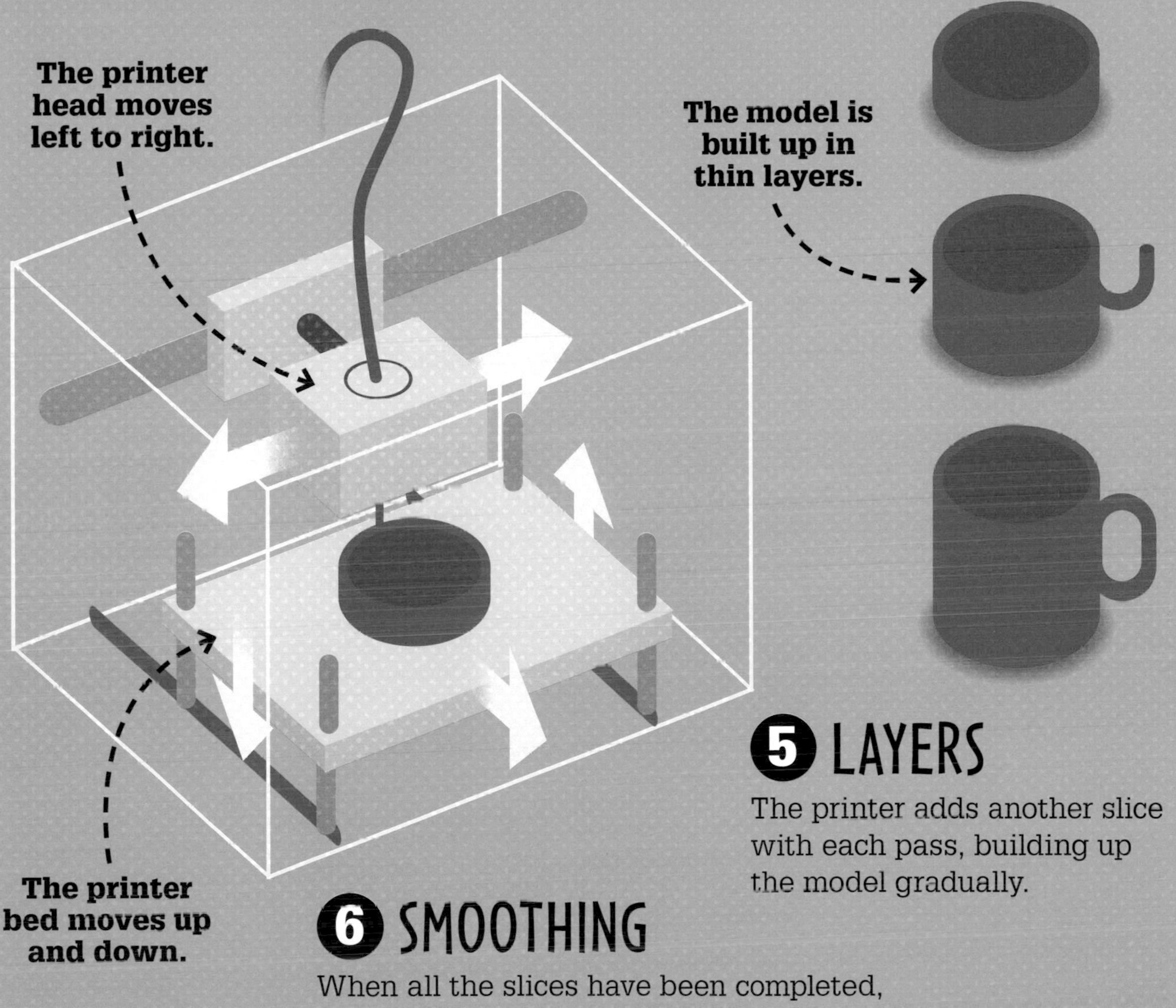

5 LAYERS

The printer adds another slice with each pass, building up the model gradually.

6 SMOOTHING

When all the slices have been completed, the model is smoothed down to remove any rough edges between the layers.

GLOSSARY

ALTITUDE
The height of something above sea level.

BASE STATION
A transmitter that is fixed in one place and is part of a mobile phone network.

BIO-GAS
A gas that can be used as a fuel and is produced when waste matter decomposes.

BROADBAND
A fast form of connection to the internet.

CAPACITIVE TOUCHSCREEN
A type of touchscreen that interprets changes in an electrical field created when someone touches the screen to input instructions.

COMPRESSOR
A device that squeezes something, increasing the pressure.

COMPUTER PROCESSOR
Also know as the Central Processing Unit, this is the part of a computer that carries out instructions from a program.

CONDENSER
A device in a refrigerator that reduces the pressure of the fluid, or refrigerant, and decreases its temperature so it can cool the inside of the refrigerator.

DIODE
An electrical device that only allows a current to flow in one direction.

DOCKING STATION
A device that connects one object to another, such as a mobile phone to a computer or a power supply.

ELECTRICAL FIELD
A field generated by an electric current.

ELECTROLUMINESCENCE
The production of light that's been created by an electric current.

ELECTROMAGNETIC SPECTRUM
The entire range of electromagnetic radiation, from radio waves with a long wavelength to gamma rays that have a very short wavelength. It includes visible light.

ELECTRONS
Tiny particles that orbit the centre, or nucleus, of an atom.

ELEMENT
A substance in its simplest form. Its atoms all have the same number of protons in their centres, or nuclei.

FIBRE-OPTIC CABLE
A cable that uses light to carry signals.

FORMAT
The form or type that something appears in.

GENERATOR
A device that turns movement into electrical energy.

GLOBAL POSITIONING SYSTEM (GPS)
A network of satellites and receivers that can give an accurate location.

GROUND SOURCE HEAT PUMP

A system that transfers heat to or from underground. It can keep a house cool in summer and warm in winter.

INFRARED

Part of the electromagnetic spectrum, with a wavelength that is longer than visible light, so it can't be seen by humans.

INSULATION

Material that can be used to reduce the flow of heat to or from an object. It can be used to keep something cool or hot.

INTERNET

The global network that allows computers to talk to each other and exchange information.

MAGNETRON

A device that produces microwaves.

MICROPHONE

A device that converts sounds into electrical energy.

MICROWAVES

Part of the electromagnetic spectrum, that can be used to heat food.

PHOTOVOLTAIC CELLS

Devices that convert sunlight into an electric current.

RADIATION

The production of energy in the form of waves or particles.

REFRIGERANT

The fluid used to cool the inside of a refrigerator.

RESISTIVE TOUCHSCREEN

A type of touchscreen, where the user presses on an upper screen so that it touches a lower screen to form a circuit.

STREAMING

Accessing information over the internet without having to download it.

THERMOSTAT

A device that controls the temperature of something.

TRANSMITTER

Something that can send radio signals.

TURBINE

A large wheel made of blades.

ULTRAVIOLET

Part of the electromagnetic spectrum, with a wavelength that is shorter than visible light. It can't be seen by humans.

ANSWERS ...

8-9 1,200 x 50 = 60,000 hours.

10-11 It takes 12.5 minutes in total, which is 750 seconds.

12-13 Your finger should feel warmer due to heat from the compressed (squeezed) air.

16-17 A normal camera would take 120 frames in 5 seconds, while a high-speed camera would take 1,250 frames. The difference is 1,130 frames.

18-19 It could store 132 movies.

22-23 9,000 ÷ 300,000 = 0.03 seconds.

INDEX

WEBSITES

www.sciencekids.co.nz/technology.html
A fun website that's packed with games, experiments, facts, videos and quizzes about science, technology and the very latest gadgets.

www.brainpop.com/technology
The technology section of a huge educational website. It includes videos, games, quizzes and activities on an enormous range of technology topics.

FOR MORE AMAZING INFOGRAPHICS, TRY THE FACT-PACKED MAPOGRAPHICA SERIES.

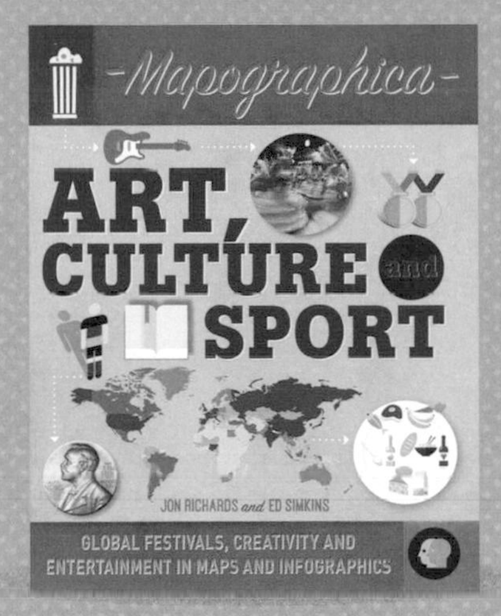

978 0 7502 9148 4

978 0 7502 9145 3

978 0 7502 9154 5

978 0 7502 9151 4

WAYLAND

www.waylandbooks.co.uk